Norman Bethune in CHINA

Adapted by Chung Chih-cheng

Illustrations by Hsu Jung-chu, Hsu Yung
Ku Lien-tang *and* Wang Yi-sheng

Fredonia Books
Amsterdam, The Netherlands

Norman Bethune in China

Adapted by Chung Chih-cheng

Illustrations by Hsu Jung-chu, Hsu Yung, Ku Lien-tang and Wang Yi-sheng

ISBN: 1-4101-0759-0

Fredonia Books
Amsterdam, The Netherlands
http://www.fredoniabooks.com

COMRADE NORMAN BETHUNE, a member of the Communist Party of Canada, was a world-famous chest surgeon. In 1937, when the War of Resistance Against Japan broke out, he was sent to China by the Communist Parties of Canada and the United States. He arrived early in 1938. In the spring of the same year he reached Yenan and was received by the great leader of the Chinese people, Chairman Mao. Soon afterwards, he went to the base area behind the enemy lines as Medical Advisor to the Shansi-Chahar-Hopei Military Area. In those hard war years he shared the joys and sorrows of the people and armymen in the Shansi-Chahar-Hopei Border Region. He adopted the cause of the Chinese people's liberation as his own. With selfless enthusiasm in his work, and imbued with the great spirit of internationalism and communism, he made a glorious contribution to the cause of the Chinese people's liberation. Unfortunately, he contracted blood poisoning while operating on wounded soldiers, and to our great sorrow, after all measures taken to cure him had proved futile, died on November 12, 1939 at Yellow Stone Village in Tang-hsien County, Hopei Province.

On December 21, 1939, Chairman Mao wrote the brilliant essay "In Memory of Norman Bethune" calling on the Chinese people to learn from Comrade Bethune. In 1940, to perpetuate his memory, the Shansi-Chahar-Hopei Military Area renamed the Model Hospital set up by him the "Bethune International Peace Hospital."

The great internationalist fighter Comrade Bethune lives forever in the hearts of millions upon millions of the Chinese people.

1. Early in 1938, after a long voyage, the great internationalist fighter Norman Bethune, who had been sent by the Communist Parties of Canada and the United States to help in the War of Resistance Against Japan, arrived in China.

2. Late in March, after a hard and hazardous journey, Comrade Bethune reached Yenan, cradle of the Chinese revolution. Here, scenes of revolutionary vitality met his eyes wherever he went. Deeply impressed, he said: "Here in Yenan I've seen new China at last!"

3. Not long after Bethune's arrival in Yenan, Chairman Mao, the great leader of the Chinese people, met him and had a friendly talk with him.

4. It was late at night. Comrade Bethune, just back from the Chairman's, was too excited to sleep. He wrote in his diary: "I now know why Mao Tsetung impresses everyone who meets him the way he does. The man is a giant! He is one of the great men of our world."

5. Comrade Bethune, clad in an 8th Route Army uniform, and bearing in mind Chairman Mao's expectations, made ready to set out for the front — the Shansi-Chahar-Hopei Border Region. On the day he was to start, the Party assigned him a bodyguard and an orderly, but Bethune said with feeling, "More comrades are needed at the front. I'll only take this one 'Little Devil' with me."

6. Comrade Bethune made a detour until he got to a ferry on the Yellow River. Medical kit in hand, he crossed the turbulent river on his way to the Shansi-Chahar-Hopei Border Region.

7.   Two months later, on June 17, Comrade Bethune reached this Border Region after a hard journey over mountains and rivers.   There he was warmly received by the people and the armymen.

8. The first question Bethune asked on entering the room was: "Where are the wounded?" The comrades urged him to rest for a few days, but he declined with a smile: "I'm here to work, not to remain idle. Please take me to the wounded men right away."

9. Early next morning, Comrade Bethune went to the rear hospital of the Military Area in Sungyenkou Village. He carefully examined the wounded one by one and inspected all the operating rooms. He found the hospital poorly equipped and badly in need of medicine. But when he saw the hard-working medical staff making medical apparatus and concocting Chinese medicine themselves, he was impressed.

10. Comrade Bethune said excitedly: "What the Chinese Communist Party has given the 8th Route Army is not superior weapons, but revolutionary fighters tempered on the Long March. With people like that as the backbone of the revolution, we have everything we need."

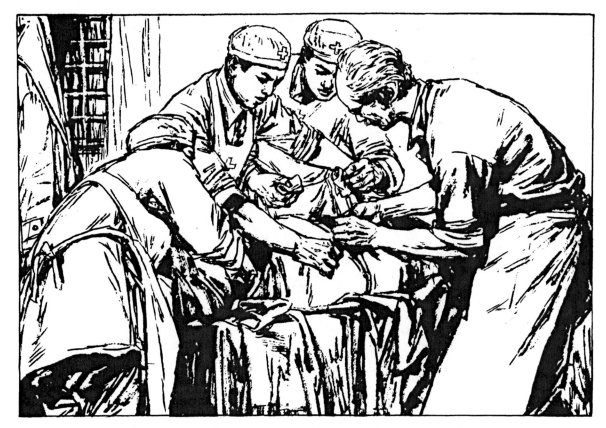

11. Comrade Bethune worked with fiery passion, examining 520 wounded men during the first week and operating on 147 within a month. Thanks to his efforts, the men soon got well and went back to the front.

12. The Military Area command brought a directive from Chairman Mao appointing Comrade Bethune medical advisor to the Military Area with a monthly allowance of 100 yuan. Comrade Bethune wrote Chairman Mao that very night, pledging to share the joys and sorrows of the people and soldiers there. The allowance he turned over to the hospital to pay for the nutrition of the wounded.

13. Even in the dead of night Comrade Bethune was still hard at work. To improve the medical service, he drew up a plan for a model hospital.

14. Soon the old temple at Sungyenkou was seething with life. At Comrade Bethune's proposal, a "Five-week Campaign" was started to convert the old poorly equipped clinic into a model hospital which would be better and more permanent. Both villagers and armymen took an active part in the campaign.

15. Comrade Bethune got busier and busier. Besides treating the wounded, he himself made drawings and taught the carpenters how to make beds and frames for treating fractures.

16. Now and then Comrade Bethune would pick up a hammer and help the blacksmiths to make medical instruments. When the comrades around asked if he used to be a worker, he said with a smile: "Well, to be a good surgeon, you have to be a blacksmith, carpenter, tailor and barber at the same time."

17. With zest Comrade Bethune gave the medical workers a series of lectures on disinfection and the treatment of wounds.

18. Members of the Village Women's Association for National Salvation volunteered to make bedding and do the washing for the hospital.

19. On the flagstone path the wounded men had to pass every day, there was a slab missing. Seeing this, Bethune, together with his comrades, put in a new slab, for he was afraid that the wounded soldiers might fall.

20. It was the day of the official opening of the Model Hospital at Sungyenkou. Military Area leaders, representatives from the Border Region government and over 2,000 people turned up to celebrate the occasion. Brimming over with enthusiasm, Comrade Bethune mounted the platform and made a speech ringing with internationalism.

21. The meeting over, Comrade Bethune enthusiastically showed people round the Model Hospital. The hospital was spick and span, and in perfect order. Though reconstructed with only the materials available on the spot, it already had the essentials of a model hospital.

22. Late in September, the Japanese invaders mobilized a force 30,000 strong, consisting of infantry, cavalry and artillery units. Backed by aircraft and mechanized troops, they launched an attack on the heart of the Border Region by ten routes.

23. An order had come for the Model Hospital to move on. On horseback, as he left Sung-yenkou, Comrade Bethune cast a lingering look at the Model Hospital to which he had devoted so much care. He said indignantly: "Damn those fascist marauders! They won't even leave us alone in our gully!"

24. Travelling over hills and mountains, Comrade Bethune passed many villages and hamlets. When he saw that the people, although menaced with the Japanese "mopping-up" campaign, were calm and militant, he was deeply moved and said to the interpreter: "The Chinese people are sure to win!"

25. The bloodthirsty Japanese invaders forced their way into Sungyenkou only to find the village deserted and the Model Hospital abandoned. All they could do was to ruthlessly burn down the empty houses. But they gained nothing, for our troops had already evaded the spearhead of the enemy forces and manoeuvred to their rear. At Shihpenkou the enemy were routed, leaving innumerable dead behind.

26. The "mopping-up" campaign was victoriously beaten back. On the way Comrade Bethune saw cartloads of captured weapons and queues of war prisoners. Overjoyed, he said, "Serves those fascists right! Please tell our men to fight more fine battles like this!"

27. Comrade Bethune earnestly studied Chairman Mao's *On Protracted War*. Greatly inspired by it, he said: "Right! What we're fighting now is a protracted people's war in a completely changed situation. There's no longer any distinction between the 'front' and the 'rear.' We must go wherever the wounded are."

28. At the end of the year, Comrade Bethune led a medical team to the village of Yang-chiachuang.

29. Along the way they were caught in a raging northwester driving before it a blinding blizzard. Bethune's moustache was white with snowflakes. He joked: "Look! I can play Santa Claus without any make-up!" They all laughed merrily.

30. The medical team crossed several high mountains without a let-up. When they finally reached Yangchiachuang, Comrade Bethune asked to start work at once.

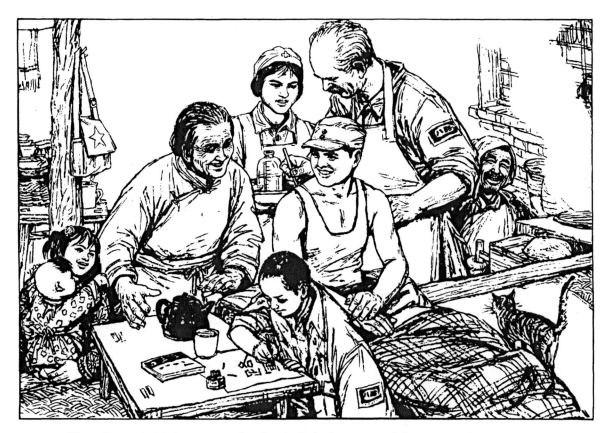

31. Here Comrade Bethune turned a local clinic into a special surgery. This kind of hospital was adapted to the characteristics of guerrilla warfare, for it used the peasants' homes as wards and their *kang* sleeping ledges as sick-beds. Deeply rooted in the midst of the masses, it could never be destroyed by the enemy.

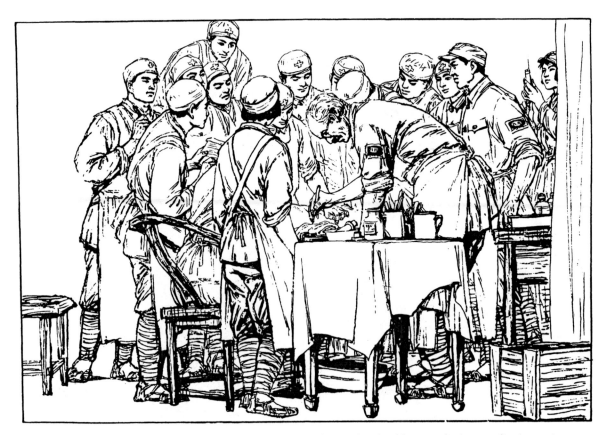

32. In order to train more medical workers to form the backbone of the medical service, Comrade Bethune started the "Practical Work Week" movement, in which the Military Area sanitary cadres were asked to join. He taught them not only by words but also by deeds. The students practised by turns, learning while working.

33. Comrade Bethune was an untiring teacher, patient and inspiring. He linked theory with practice and made his lectures vivid and easy to understand.

34. During the break Comrade Bethune used to ask the students to "shave" and incise gourds so as to improve their skill in using the scalpel for operations on human skulls.

35. To improve their technique in anaesthesia, Comrade Bethune once asked the students to experiment in using a general instead of local anaesthetic when opening an abscess on his toe.

36. The students could not but comply with his request. After the operation, Comrade Bethune smiled. "You see, if you co-ordinate the anaesthesia and operation, well, it can shorten the time of anaesthetization. In this way you can do a lot to ease the suffering of the wounded." Everyone was greatly inspired by Comrade Bethune's spirit of constantly perfecting medical skills.

37. The "Practical Work Week" soon came to an end. The trainees found it hard to tear themselves away from Comrade Bethune. They had benefited a lot from the pains he had taken. They said: "We've learned more in seven days than we could in seven months of book study."

38. "To the front! To the wounded!" At Bethune's suggestion, a mobile field medical team was set up. Day and night its members pressed forward along rough, steep mountain paths and were always ready to serve the wounded, even in the thick of the battle.

39. To meet the particular requirements of guerrilla warfare, Bethune tried to improve the method of carrying medicine and medical equipment. One day he happened to see a villager coming along with a donkey. Slung across its back was a pair of panniers filled with manure. Bethune shouted happily, "Hurray, I've got it."

40. With the panniers as a model, Bethune devised a bridge-shaped container that could hold everything needed for an operating room and a dressing station. It could serve as a table for dressing wounds when unfolded. And when folded up it could be carried like saddle-bags. All the comrades spoke highly of this invention.

41. Without caring for his own safety, Comrade Bethune led the mobile medical team to the front, where they would often work in the midst of the battle.

42. In February 1939, a fierce battle was reported in central Hopei. Comrade Bethune asked to be sent there. The request was granted immediately. Soon an "East Expeditionary Medical Team" was formed. It headed for central Hopei.

43. Across the vast plain of central Hopei the name of Dr. Bethune went from mouth to mouth. One night in April, when a battle had started at Chihui, Comrade Bethune took the medical team to Wenchiatun, a village only three and a half kilometres from the battle front. Here in a small temple he soon had the operating room ready for the wounded.

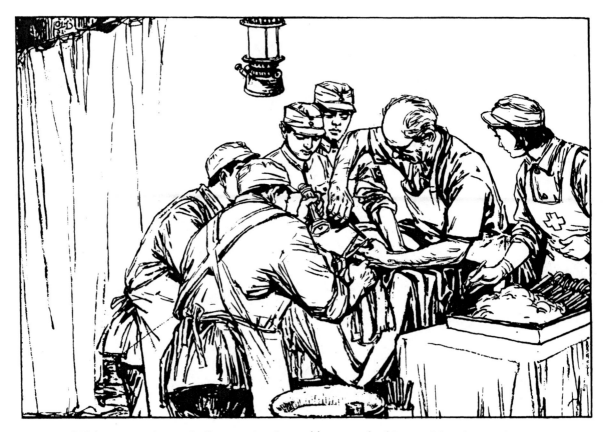

44. With enemy planes circling overhead, machine-guns barking and hand-grenades bursting all round, Comrade Bethune concentrated all his attention on the wounded. He had been working like that for two days and nights on end.

45. Boom! A bomb suddenly exploded near the temple. The whole building shook violently and the back wall crumbled.

46. Dr. Bethune's comrades urged him to take shelter, but he refused, saying: "In making revolution, in fighting the fascists, no one should think of his own safety. A Communist Party member must never put himself first."

47. Night fell and Bethune was still at his operating table. He had been working there without a break for a long time. Tears of anxiety came into the eyes of his orderly, who had heated his supper over and over again.

48. In the battle, a Company Commander Hsu was seriously wounded in the stomach while leading a heroic charge against the enemy.

49. In spite of the acute pain, Company Commander Hsu remained at his post till victory was won.

50. The stretcher-bearers took Hsu to the operating room for immediate treatment. When Bethune found that Hsu's intestines had been pierced in ten places, he said admiringly to his comrades, "He's a good, daring lad. I feel happy and honoured to be able to serve fighters like him."

51. The battle ended in victory. In the rush to rescue the wounded, Dr. Bethune worked for three days and nights without rest. Because of his timely treatment, 85 per cent of the wounded recovered. He said happily: "Time means life for our class brothers."

52. Comrade Bethune escorted Hsu and several other badly wounded soldiers to the rear hospital. On the way he would now and then ask about how they were feeling. When the men, full of gratitude, replied: "Fine!" Bethune said with a broad smile, "When you tell me you're fine, I've nothing to worry about."

53. In the rear hospital, Bethune rigged up a backrest for Company Commander Hsu. He said to the other doctors: "A man wounded in the belly finds it hard to breathe. This way he'll be more comfortable."

54. Every day Comrade Bethune personally prepared four meals for Hsu. When the cook offered to do the job, he said, "I think I'd better do it myself, as I know my patients better. Medical treatment isn't all that's necessary. When a suitable diet is combined with it, recovery is quicker."

55. When the food was ready, Comrade Bethune would bring it to Company Commander Hsu. Spoon-feeding him, he would say, "Here, another bite. When you pull through, you'll be able to kill more enemy soldiers." With tears in his eyes, Company Commander Hsu could hardly find words to express his gratitude.

56. Thanks to Bethune's meticulous treatment and care, Hsu soon got well and was ready to go back to the front. On leaving, Hsu said, his eyes brimming over with tears, "Dr. Bethune, when I get back to the front, I'll kill more of the enemy."

57. One day a severely wounded soldier who was to undergo an amputation urgently needed a blood transfusion. All the comrades volunteered to offer him blood.

58. But Comrade Bethune shook his head, saying, "You donated your blood only a couple of days ago. It's my turn now. My blood type is Universal Group O, good for any patient." When he stretched out his arm the comrades said: "That won't do. Think of your age. . . ." Comrade Bethune said: "Listen. Our men at the front are ready to shed all their blood for the country and the people. I think I ought to give some of mine, too."

59. Comrade Bethune lay down beside the wounded soldier and said: "Come on! There's no time to lose in rescuing the wounded!" So the blood of Comrade Norman Bethune, proletarian internationalist fighter and worthy son of the Canadian people, ran into the veins of the Chinese fighter and saved his life.

60. The story of Comrade Bethune giving his blood to a wounded 8th Route Armyman soon spread far and wide. A volunteer Blood Donor Corps was quickly organized by the masses. Deeply moved, Comrade Bethune said: "The masses are our blood bank. This is something unknown in the history of surgery."

61. Towards the end of April, Comrade Bethune learned that a few dozen wounded 8th Route Armymen were hidden in Ssukung Village near the enemy blockade line. He offered to go and look after them. As it was a danger spot where the enemy might turn up at any moment, the leadership tried to talk him out of it, but in vain. Finally it was decided that the medical team should set off at night, with an escort unit.

62. The team got to Ssukung Village safely. Comrade Bethune had been busy the whole day, but there was still a lot left to do. At night, in order to be on guard against any surprise attack by the enemy, Comrade Bethune and his men slept with their clothes on, and kept their horses saddled, so that they could move off at a moment's notice.

63. At dawn the next day, a peasant came across a group of enemy soldiers to the west of the village. One shouted at him, "Where's Ssukung Village?" The peasant shrewdly pointed northwest: "It's over there!" Having thus misdirected the enemy, he ran as fast as he could back to the village and told the medical team what had happened.

64. In a quarter of an hour or so the medical team was out of Ssukung and the wounded were safely hidden by the people. Comrade Bethune said with feeling: "The 8th Route Army is like fish in the ocean of the people. An army like that is invincible!"

65. For four months Comrade Bethune worked in the central Hopei plain, leaving a profound impression on the people and armymen there. The Party Committee of the Shansi-Chahar-Hopei Border Region invited him to attend the coming Party Congress as an observer. Comrade Bethune, gladly accepting the invitation, hurried back to western Hopei.

66. One evening the medical team came to a village near enemy-occupied Chingfengtien. They were about to break through the blockade line when Bethune came across a peasant who had a pus infection in his chest. He promptly told his comrades to halt, so that he could operate at once.

67. The village was very close to the Peiping-Hankow Railway, then tightly blockaded by enemy troops. For security's sake the escort troops sealed off this area with the help of the local underground Party organization. It took Dr. Bethune only 20 minutes to finish the operation. As everything came off satisfactory, the peasant was overwhelmed with gratitude.

68. Escorted by the masses, the medical team succeeded in running the blockade.

69. On July 1, Comrade Bethune attended the Party Congress of the Border Region. At the meeting he said passionately, "The war you are waging is a just one. You are by no means alone. The people all over the world are on your side. . . ."

70. Not long afterwards Comrade Bethune moved to Shenpei Village where he worked day and night on *A Manual of Organization and Technique for Divisional Field Hospitals in Guerrilla War*. The book, written in the light of Chairman Mao's strategic thinking, summed up experience of medical treatment on the battlefield. It was a valuable gift to the Chinese people.

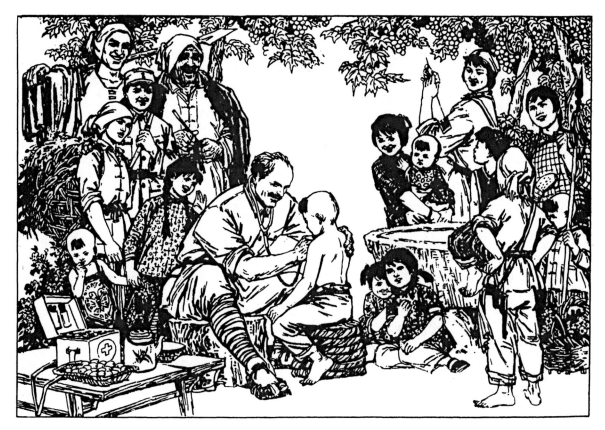

71. Though always on the move in this wartime situation, Comrade Bethune gave medical care not only to the wounded soldiers but also to the people. So the people affectionately called him "Our Doctor Bethune."

72. One day, Dr. Bethune went to Hochiachuang. Before entering the village, he saw a peasant with a badly swollen arm that bothered him terribly. He went right up to the peasant and took him to the clinic.

73. When the operation was over, Comrade Bethune said to the peasant: "Please tell the villagers I'm a doctor of the 8th Route Army. Tell them to come to me whenever they are ill."

74. Two days later Comrade Bethune called at the peasant's home to give his arm a new dressing. The peasant said with deep emotion: "Oh, Dr. Bethune, I don't know how to thank you enough." Bethune promptly replied: "No need to thank me. It's the 8th Route Army you should thank."

75. The villager, having recovered, brought some red dates and eggs for Comrade Bethune. He tried to refuse these gifts, but as the villager insisted, had to accept some of them. Later, he told a nurse to take the dates and eggs to the wounded.

76. One day, on hearing that there was a seriously wounded soldier on the verge of death in a village some 25 kilometres away, Comrade Bethune jumped on his horse and rode off at full gallop.

77. It was already dusk when Comrade Bethune finished the operation. As he remember-
ed that there were some other wounded waiting to be operated on, he mounted the horse,
which was still damp with sweat, and hastened back at once.

78. The leading cadres were very concerned about Comrade Bethune's health. One day they had some chicken soup especially prepared for him. But when the orderly brought him two bowls of the soup, he took them to the wounded soldiers. The orderly was very worried, but Comrade Bethune said, "I am a communist fighter. How can I enjoy any special privileges!"

79. Late at night, Comrade Bethune would go on his rounds of the wards, lamp in hand. He would see for himself that the wounded soldiers were sleeping well and properly covered.

80. In those hard days Comrade Bethune, like any ordinary 8th Route Armyman, always had his sewing-kit with him, and mended his own clothes.

81. A young soldier already well and about to return to his unit presented Comrade Bethune with a pair of straw sandals he had made himself. Comrade Bethune accepted them gladly. "What a precious gift!" he said, putting them on.

82. Comrade Bethune decided to take a short trip home to Canada. His purpose was to tell the whole world about the great War of Resistance being waged by the Chinese people against Japan and to make a public appeal for funds, medicine and medical supplies.

83. Comrade Bethune was scheduled to leave on October 20, 1939. But just at this time the Japanese invaders began a large-scale winter "mopping-up" campaign in the mountain regions of western Hopei. Comrade Bethune promptly postponed his departure and led the mobile team to the Laiyuan-Motienling front, where fierce fighting was going on.

84. Near Sunchiachuang Village, about four kilometres from the front, the medical team met some wounded soldiers brought in from Motienling (Sky-Kissing Peak). Without even taking time to eat, Bethune and his comrades set about improvising an operating theatre in a small temple on the hillside and started work at once.

85. On the second afternoon of the attack, while Comrade Bethune was busy at work, a sentinel ran in and reported that enemy soldiers were on the hill opposite.

86. Comrade Bethune asked in a calm voice, "How many wounded men haven't been operated on yet?" "Ten," answered his comrades. Comrade Bethune issued rapid orders: "Get two more operating tables ready right away. Let's try and finish the operations as fast as we can."

87. They worked energetically on three patients at a time. A few minutes later, the sentinel came in and reported: "The enemy have come down the hill." But Comrade Bethune kept on operating as if he had heard nothing at all.

88. Suddenly rifle shots rang out in the valley down below. The sentinel ran in and said: "The company of guards are now engaging the enemy." When the interpreter urged him to leave right away Comrade Bethune said in a firm voice: "An army doctor's duty is to stay with the fighters and never leave them. If he dies at his post, it's a glorious death."

89.   Twenty minutes later, the last patient, wounded in the leg, was brought in and laid on Comrade Bethune's operating table.   Rifle fire rang out again, this time at closer range. The sentinel rushed in and gave the alarm: "The enemy are approaching the village."

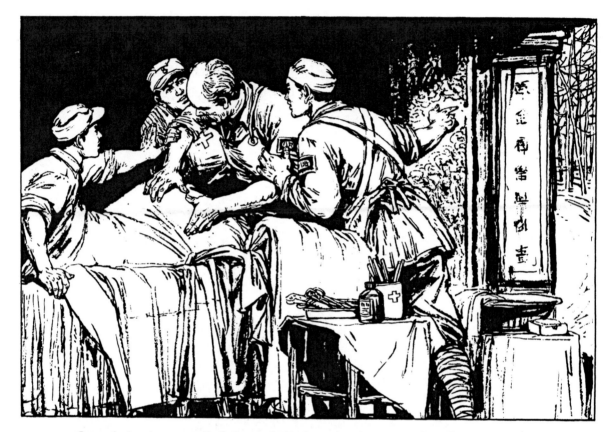

90. One of the doctors pulled Comrade Bethune by the arm and said, "Let me take your place. You must leave at once." Comrade Bethune, pushing the doctor's hand aside, said to the anaesthetist: "Local anaesthesia!" The wounded soldier raised his head and pleaded: "Please go, Doctor Bethune. It's not a bad wound. . . . Please go before the enemy comes."

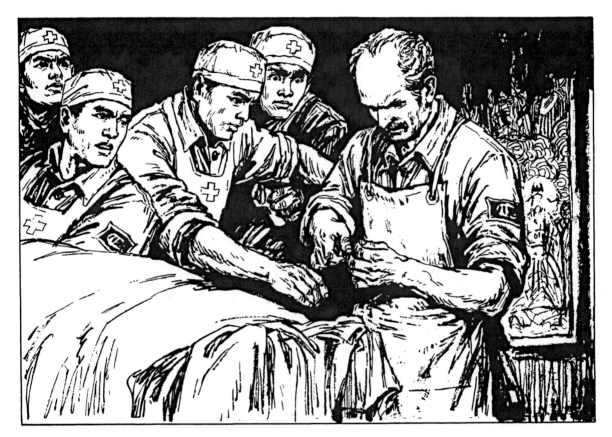

91. Comrade Bethune was swiftly doing the operation when suddenly he whispered, as if to himself, "Damn!" Everybody turned round only to see blood oozing down the middle finger of his left hand. "It's nothing," he said, "I just cut myself with my scalpel." He dipped his finger into tincture of iodine and then went back to his work.

92. The sharp rattle of machine-gun shots, like hailstones on cold steel, came nearer and nearer. When he finished the last stitch, Comrade Bethune took a deep breath and said: "Take him away!" In no time he was in the saddle, and galloping down the hill.

93. On the way the comrades remarked that they had had a close shave, but Comrade Bethune said with a smile: "We've won a great victory today. Eighth Route Armymen aren't afraid of whizzing bullets and bursting shells, and don't leave the front when lightly wounded. I am a medical advisor of the 8th Route Army. So I shouldn't, either."

94. The medical team kept riding the whole night until they came to the rear hospital at Kanhoching. Comrade Bethune's finger had become inflamed, so the comrades advised him to rest. He said: "Thank you, comrades, for your concern. But there are so many wounded in need of treatment. How can I sit idly by?" So he worked busily for another two days on end.

95. Unfortunately, while Comrade Bethune was giving emergency treatment to a wounded soldier with erysipelas, his finger became infected. A few days later, it became swollen and festered, and his temperature rose to 39.6 degrees Centigrade. The comrades were all very anxious about him. "It's nothing," he said, "you needn't worry! I could go on working even if I had only two fingers left."

96. Still half asleep, Comrade Bethune heard the booming of cannon. He knew there was a battle going on. He rushed out of the room, insisting that he should go to the front. When the comrades urged him to stay, he said hotly: "I have an infected finger, nothing more! What does it matter? You should use me like a machine-gun."

97. The leading cadres and comrades could not talk him out of it, so the medical team, braving the sleet, set out for the front. Comrade Bethune mounted his horse but rocked precariously in the saddle, feeling faint and weak.

98. The roar of the guns came nearer and nearer. On the way, the medical team met the wounded soldiers brought in from the Huangtuling front. Comrade Bethune hurried up to them and said apologetically: "Sorry to be late! Sorry to be so late!"

99. When they arrived at Wangchiatai, where a regimental medical team was stationed, they saw that Comrade Bethune's illness had become more serious. The infection had spread and an abscess had formed near his elbow joint. However, he insisted that the wounded soldiers, especially those injured in the head, the chest, or the stomach, be brought to him for treatment. He asked the comrades to wake him up if he was asleep.

100. Weak as he was, Comrade Bethune still managed to work for another 16 hours without a break. He refused to rest, although the comrades had asked him time and again to do so. Everybody was moved to tears by the enthusiasm with which he worked.

101. On November 9, Comrade Bethune's condition got worse. His temperature rose to 40 degrees Centigrade. As the enemy resumed their attack on Wangchiatai, the army leadership decided to evacuate at once. The leading comrades of the unit came to see Comrade Bethune and insisted that he should return to the rear for treatment. It was with great reluctance that Comrade Bethune finally agreed.

102. On the way Comrade Bethune shivered all over with cold, occasionally vomiting. But he still kept looking back in the direction of the front and said: "What I'm worried about most are the fighters shedding their blood at the front. If I had any strength left in me I would remain there."

103. On November 10, Comrade Bethune arrived at Yellow Stone Village in Tanghsien County, where his condition grew ever graver. When the Military Area command heard of this, they immediately gave an urgent order: Comrade Bethune must be saved at all costs!

104. Doctors specially sent by the Military Area command came post-haste to Yellow Stone Village to help save Comrade Bethune.

105. When the villagers learned that Comrade Bethune was getting worse, they gathered in the courtyard to wait for further news. Darkness fell, but nobody would leave.

106. When a detachment of troops passing through Yellow Stone Village learned that Comrade Bethune was lying ill, they all rushed over to see him.

107. The officers and men crowded before the window of Comrade Bethune's room. When they saw the critical state he was in, tears streamed down their faces. Clasping the doctors' hands they said: "Please do everything possible to cure him! We will help you to cure him. By fighting hard. He'll be glad to hear the good news of victory. . . ."

108. The doctors took all the emergency measures they could, but there was no sign of improvement in Comrade Bethune's condition. The doctors suggested amputation of the infected arm. Comrade Bethune shook his head and said: "I trust you, but you'd better give up, for mine is a hopeless case. . . . It is no longer a matter of the arm. . . . It's in the blood. Septicemia. Nothing can help me."

109. On the night of November 11, Comrade Bethune summoned his last strength to sit up in bed, and began to write a letter to the Military Area command, including a message to be passed on to the Communist Party of Canada and the American people: "I have been very happy. My only regret is that I shall now be unable to do more.... The last two years have been the most significant, the most meaningful years of my life. . . ."

110. Late at night, looking at the comrades around him, Comrade Bethune said with emotion: "Please convey to Chairman Mao my thanks for the education he and the Communist Party of China have given me. I am deeply convinced that the Chinese people will win their liberation. The pity is that I shall not be able to see for myself the birth of a new China."

111. Holding the hand of one of the doctors, Comrade Bethune gasped out these words: "Organize a medical team, go near the front, and take in the wounded. . . ." With tears in their eyes, the doctors assured him that everything had been arranged, and they asked him to rest well.

112. With his head raised high, Comrade Bethune uttered his last words in a firm voice: "Fight on! Continue along the great road and carry the cause forward!"

113. In the early morning of November 12, 1939, Comrade Norman Bethune, the great internationalist fighter, laid down his precious life while working for the cause of the Chinese people's liberation. When the sad tidings reached the front, the fighters shouted loudly, "Let's avenge our Doctor Bethune!" and charged the enemy positions with renewed force.

114. On December 21, 1939, Chairman Mao wrote the brilliant essay "In Memory of Norman Bethune" calling on the Chinese people to learn from him. In 1952, the remains of Comrade Bethune were moved to the North China Martyrs' Cemetery in Shihchiachuang City, Hopei. Comrade Bethune, the great internationalist fighter, will live forever in the hearts of millions upon millions of the Chinese people.

Printed in the United States
99528LV00006B/171/A